EGG THOUGHTS
And Other Frances Songs

by RUSSELL HOBAN
Pictures by LILLIAN HOBAN

HarperCollinsPublishers

Egg Thoughts
And Other Frances Songs
Text copyright © 1964, 1972 by Russell Hoban
Illustrations copyright © 1972, 1994 by Lillian Hoban

Library of Congress Cataloging-in-Publication Data
Hoban, Russell.
 Egg thoughts, and other Frances songs / by Russell Hoban ; pictures
by Lillian Hoban.
  p.   cm.
 Summary: Twenty-two poems reflect Frances' observations on the
events in her life.
  ISBN 0-06-022331-6. — ISBN 0-06-022332-4 (lib. bdg.)
  ISBN 0-06-443378-1 (pbk.)
  [1. American poetry.]   I. Hoban, Lillian, ill.   II. Title.
[PZ8.H63Eg   1994]   92-44004
811'.5'4—dc20   CIP
                                                                        AC

1 2 3 4 5 6 7 8 9 10
❖
Newly Illustrated Edition

For Here and Now,
with love

SONGS

EGG THOUGHTS

Soft-Boiled

I do not like the way you slide,
I do not like your soft inside,
I do not like you many ways,
And I could do for many days
Without a soft-boiled egg.

Sunny-Side-Up

With their yolks and whites all runny
They are looking at me funny.

Sunny-Side-Down

Lying face-down on the plate
On their stomachs there they wait.

Poached

Poached eggs on toast, why do you shiver
With such a funny little quiver?

Scrambled

I eat as well as I am able,
But some falls underneath the table.

Hard-Boiled

With so much suffering today
Why do them any other way?

SOME KIDS I KNOW

I know kids who do not kick
Stones down roads or even pick
Sea-glass up on beaches.

I know kids who when they get
Brand-new boots won't get them wet—
They won't walk through puddles.

When they have some jelly beans
They don't care if reds or greens
Are the ones they eat first.

If they get a shiny penny
They don't care—it isn't any
Difference to them.
Kids like that just simply do not care.

STRING

Balls of string or little bits
Of it in your pocket, it's
What I call a cozy thing
Always to have lots of string.

Summer, winter, fall and spring,
All the seasons have their string.

Sometimes when I lose a kite
Far away and out of sight,
Then the string that I rewind
As I walk until I find
Where my kite is, takes me through
Places I might not get to
If I didn't like string.

STONE-KICKING SONG

Beginning

Mister Stone, all alone,
Waiting for someone to pick him—
Mister Stone has his own
Friends who come along and kick him.

Middle

Down the road, fast and slow,
Kicking Mister Stone I go.

Almost the End

Mister Stone never talks rolling down the middle
Of the road, but in streams he will sing a little.

The End

There's the water, running fast;
This is where I kick him last.
Good-bye, Mister Stone.

STUPID OLD MYSELF

Stupid old myself today
Found a four leaf clover,
Left it where it blew away,
All my good luck's over.
Done and finished, gone astray
Stupid old myself today.

Stupid with a brand new kite
Lost it in a tree
Way up high and tangled tight—
No more kite for me.

12

Stupid falling off a log
When I tried to get
Close enough to catch a frog
Came home very wet.

Then I swapped my teddy bear
In a stupid muddle
For a doll that's lost her hair.
No more bear to cuddle.

Walking slowly and alone
Stupid and in sorrow
I just found a lucky stone—
Maybe I'll be smart tomorrow.
With today one day behind me
Maybe my good luck will find me.

LORNA DOONE
LAST COOKIE SONG
(I SHARED IT WITH GLORIA)

All the sandwich cookies sweet
In their frilly paper neat,
They are gone this afternoon,
They have left you, Lorna Doone.

Lorna Doone, Lorna Doone,
Roaming through the heather,
Lorna Doone, Lorna Doone,
We'll grow old together.

Chocolate and vanilla creams
Pass like little tasty dreams,
Eaten up and gone too soon,
All but you, our Lorna Doone.

You are plain and you are square
And your flavor's only fair.
Soon there'll be an empty place
Where we saw your smiling face.

Lorna Doone, Lorna Doone,
You were last but you weren't wasted.
Lorna Doone, Lorna Doone,
We'll remember how you tasted.

NA-NA DOLL

My one-eyed friend, my Na-Na Doll,
Is not too big and not too small,
She's just exactly right.

Her seams are split, her plush is worn,
Her tail is limp, her apron's torn,
She isn't very bright.

But she's my friend, my tried-and-true.
She's better than a doll that's new
To sleep with every night.

If I lost her, I'd never name
Another doll like her the same.
I'd call the new one Nee-Nee.

MY LOST NOAH'S ARK

Noah's ark, Noah's ark,
Lost and lonesome in the dark,
Don't know where to find you.

In the closet you are not,
Noah's ark I haven't got,
Nowhere in the closet.

Camels, lions, tigers, donkeys,
Elephants, gazelles, and monkeys
Are not in the basement.

One of my old teddy bears
Lives behind the attic stairs.
I know where to find him.

My lost marble, I can find it
In the tool shed or behind it
When I need that marble.

Mister Noah, Noah's wife,
What will you do all your life
If I do not find you?

Are you over, are you under
Something else? The rain and thunder,
Can you hear them there?

Mister Noah in your ark,
Lost and lonesome in the dark,
Are the animals all right?
Do you tuck them in at night?
Will I ever find you?

FUNERAL

Gloria and I have often,
Walking slowly, singing steady,
With a shoebox for a coffin,
Buried neighbors who were ready.

Harold Woodmouse, Bertha Toad
(One a cat killed, one a dog)
On the hillside near the road
Sleep along with Herman Frog.

In our funeral today,
Going to his final rest:
Buster William Henry Jay,
Fallen lately from the nest.

Not quite old enough to fly,
Barely big enough to die—
In the hillside here we lay
Buster William Henry Jay.

SONGS FOR TELEVISION SHOWS
I WOULD LIKE TO SEE

Doctor Vampire

Why are all the dogs so nervous,
Why do people howl with fright,
What's he carrying in his thermos,
Where's he hurrying in the night?
Doctor Vampire!

Mister Skeleton

In a phone booth right this minute
Hangs a skin with no one in it.
If a phone call breaks your slumber
Mister Skeleton has your number.
Ho ho ho ho. Ho ho ho.

MY FRIEND THELMA

Such a friend as my friend Thelma everyone has not.
Such a friend as my friend Thelma is who I have got.

She's the one who always knows
In the winter when it snows
That the school bus will get through,
Calls up kids like me and you
So that we won't think the bus
Isn't coming. Hopeful us.

Thelma, when the ice is new,
Always says, "I think that you
Ought to try it," and I do,
And it's thin, and I go through.
When I get home sopping wet,
Into trouble's what I get.

Thelma will drop in on me
When I have friends, two or three,
Playing dolls and having fun.
Thelma is the extra one
Who is there when she should be
Somewhere else and not with me.

I have seen her several times
With an uncle who gives dimes
Going to the movies. They will take
Other friends, and they have cake
Topped with ice cream after. All good chances
Go to other friends than Frances.

My friend Thelma is a pain but one that I can stay with.
I know people who have even worse than her to play with.

NOT-THINGS

I know how, I know how, I know how to not-do things.
I know how to not-wash dishes,
I know how to not-catch fishes,
I know how to not-play ball,
I know how to not-do all
Kinds of things. I have had
No-tea parties. They're not bad.
I have flown big red no-kites,
I have taken juicy no-bites
Out of apples that weren't there.

Sometimes it is not a dumb thing,
Sometimes it is really something,
Doing no-thing.

CHOCOLATE

Why did I forget the chocolate
I was saving in my pocket
When my blue jeans went into the washer?

TELEPHONE POLE
STONE-THROWING SONG

While you're holding up your wires
Lonesome and alone
I will come to visit you
And throw a friendly stone.

BEES

Honeybees are very tricky—
Honey doesn't make them sticky.

A GLORIA SONG
(BY GLORIA)

I pick frogs and I catch flowers
At the pond for hours and hours.
I gave Mother yesterday
A hopping daisy-frog bouquet.

GLORIA, MY LITTLE SISTER

Gloria, my little sister—
Well, I guess I would have missed her
If there hadn't ever been a
Gloria my little sister.

She's the one they all like better,
She's the one that gets the most.
When she stays up late they let her
Make a mess with cinnamon toast.
I get spanked if I just twist her
Arm, that little Gloria sister.
Still, I guess I would have missed her.

No one ever thinks she's tricky.
She spilled honey on the floor—
Mother found me very sticky.
Gloria was out the door.
When I caught her no one hit her.
I got spanked because I bit her
Ear, that little Gloria sister.
Still, I guess I would have missed her.

She can hardly throw a ball,
She can't ever catch at all.
Father said that I was mean
When my ball went through the screen
Door because she stepped aside.
Mother kissed her when she cried.
I was sorry that I missed her,
Gloria my little sister.

Brothers would have been all right.
Brothers help you in a fight,
Brothers put your worms on hooks,
Brothers lend you comic books.
Why can't fathers, why can't mothers
Give us large and useful brothers?
Still, I guess I would have missed her,
Gloria my little sister.

SUMMER GOES

Summer goes, summer goes
Like the sand between my toes
When the waves go out.
That's how summer pulls away,
Leaves me standing here today,
Waiting for the school bus.

Summer brought, summer brought
All the frogs that I have caught,
Frogging at the pond,
Hot dogs, flowers, shells and rocks,
Postcards in my postcard box—
Places far away.

Summer took, summer took
All the lessons in my book,
Blew them far away.
I forgot the things I knew—
Arithmetic and spelling too,
Never thought about them.

Summer's gone, summer's gone—
Fall and winter coming on,
Frosty in the morning.
Here's the school bus right on time.
I'm not really sad that I'm
Going back to school.

HOMEWORK

Homework sits on top of Sunday, squashing Sunday flat.
Homework has the smell of Monday, homework's very fat
Heavy books and piles of paper, answers I don't know.
Sunday evening's almost finished, now I'm going to go
Do my homework in the kitchen. Maybe just a snack,
Then I'll sit right down and start as soon as I run back
For some chocolate sandwich cookies. Then I'll really do
All that homework in a minute. First I'll see what new
Show they've got on television in the living room.
Everybody's laughing there, but misery and gloom
And a full refrigerator are where I am at.
I'll just have another sandwich. Homework's very fat.

WINDOWS

When you look before you go
Outside in the rain or snow,
It looks colder, it looks wetter
Through the window. It is better
When you're outside in it.

When you're out and it's still light
Even though it's almost night
And your mother at the door
Calls you in, there is no more
Daylight in the window when you're inside looking out.

SICK IN WINTER

Winter's when your clothes are wet
A lot of times, and if you get
Sick enough to stay in bed
With coughing, sneezing, and your head
All coldsy, it is not so bad. I'm
Never sick in summertime.

Winter breakfasts when you're sick
You have in bed—the oatmeal's thick
With raisins, and poached eggs on toast
(Which once I did not like)—almost
I'm glad when Mother brings them up
With orange juice, and then a cup
Of chocolate, which I like the best
With whipped cream on it. Then I rest.
My dolls get sick along with me,
And while I'm resting they have tea.

The afternoons are slow and long.
I read my books and sing a song
Of drowsy winter noses blowing,
And fall asleep and see it's snowing
When I wake. Then Father comes to visit me,
And after dinner, rose-hip tea
And story-time. Then, tucked in tight,
My cold and I are kissed goodnight.

In the morning, snug and dry,
I wake to see my friends go by
Through snow and rain to go to school.
I wave to them and wonder who'll
Be next to stay home for a while
And lie in bed and sneeze and smile
And through their window see me go
To school through all the rain and snow.

ONE BIG RAIN

One big rain, one big rain
Made the trees all black and bare,
Showed us winter standing there.

One big rain, one big rain
Brings the green all back again,
New spring puddles in the lane
I can see my face in.